A PLEASANT PLACE

Encouraging Thoughts for the Heart

Compiled by
ALICE GRAY

Art by
KATIA ANDREEVA

BLUE COTTAGE GIFTS™
a Division of Multnomah Publishers, Inc.
Sisters, Oregon

A PLEASANT PLACE:
Encouraging Thoughts for the Heart

© 2001 by Blue Cottage Gifts™
Published by Blue Cottage Gifts™, a division of Multnomah Publishers, Inc.®
P.O. Box 1720, Sisters, OR 97759

ISBN 1-58860-006-8

Artwork by Katia Andreeva
Artwork designs by Katia are reproduced under license from Koechel Peterson & Associates, Minneapolis,
MN. and may not be reproduced without permission. For information regarding art prints featured in
this book, please contact:
   Koechel Peterson & Associates
   2600 E. 26th St.
   Minneapolis, MN 55406
   1-612-721-5017

Designed by Koechel Peterson & Associates, Minneapolis, Minnesota

Multnomah Publishers, Inc. has made every effort to trace the ownership of all poems and quotes. In the
event of a question arising from the use of a poem or quote, we regret any error made and will be pleased
to make the necessary correction in future editions of this book.

Please see the acknowledgments at the back of the book for complete attributions for this material.

Scripture quotations are taken from the *New American Standard Bible* (NASB) © 1977, 1995
by the Lockman Foundation used by permission, and *The Holy Bible*, New International Version (NIV)
© 1973, 1984 by International Bible Society, used by permission of Zondervan Publishing House.

Printed in China

01 02 03 04 05 06 — 10 9 8 7 6 5 4 3 2 1 0

www.gift-talk.com

CONTENTS

A PLEASANT PLACE

We pass through life together, you and I, along a winding journey of days and years. Though the way seems long at times, special turns of our path may reveal quiet corners of beauty. Our hearts long to linger in such places…to rest…to feel the warmth of the morning sun…to hear a robin's song from a blossomed branch…to breathe in the fragrance of a newly opened rose, jeweled with dew.

Encouragement is such a place…a place where we would pause in our travels. The kind words and deeds of loving friends are like sun-splashes at our feet, like soft spring showers that sweeten the air, like tiny wayside gardens of bright flowers, touching the heart with their simple beauty.

To receive (and give!) such encouragement is one of the choice privileges of life. Just to think that a few well-chosen words—or a simple act of thoughtful kindness—could change the course of someone's day. What an awesome thought! The truth is, our gentle, caring acts reach out to hurting hearts like a warm embrace. Those little deeds of watchful tenderness are delicate blooms along the trail, cheering and lending courage to a weary soul.

May the stories in this little book part the clouds of your day, bringing a shaft of sunlight and a warm surge of hope. And if you find encouragement…don't forget to pass it along.

KINDNESS

Author unknown • from In The Company of Friends

I have wept in the night for the shortness of sight

That to somebody's need made me blind;

But I never have yet felt a tinge of regret

For being a little too kind.

*Live for something…do good, and leave behind
you a monument of virtue that the storms of time
can never destroy. Write your name in kindness,
love and mercy on the hearts of thousands you
come in contact with year by year and you will
never be forgotten. Your name and good deed will
shine as the stars of heaven.*

THOMAS CHALMERS

BEAUTY CONTEST

Allison Harms

I won a beauty contest when I was in third grade. I didn't expect to. At nine years old, I already knew that my face was too full, that my eyes were set too closely together, that the angles of my chin and nose were too sharp. Besides, I wore glasses and my teeth were crooked. My body could not be called a "figure" except in geometric terms: I was a flat rectangle with a building block build. In addition to all my physical drawbacks, my older sister had informed me that I had the personality of overcooked cauliflower.

On the day of the contest, all these negative appraisals compounded my fears as I stood to be judged against a whole civilization of more beautiful girls. They had all arrived at school giggling in new dresses, shiny black patent leather shoes, curls, ribbons—even lipstick. I'm sure my dress was fine too and that my mother had done her best with my belligerently straight hair. I'd worn those pink sponge rollers overnight so at least my hair was doing something under my droopy ribbon. Still, I felt like I was facing a firing squad as the other classes filed in to watch the spectacle, laughing and pointing. When the teacher began to list the names of the contestants, I concentrated on trying to make time fast-forward so that I could avoid this moment. I imagined being home curled up in my reading chair with my book and my cat. Drinking cocoa and eating warm cinnamon toast. Another part of my mind was already comforting my soon-to-be-rejected self. "This doesn't matter," I told myself. "The judges aren't fair. They're just going to pick the teacher's pet."

A sudden hush interrupted all the pictures and voices in my head. Then my teacher's voice, my name, and loud cheers and clapping from the crowd. A small, rough ceramic disc was placed in my hand. As I translated the words scratched into its surface, that hard, red clay became a treasure in my hand. I read: "Allison—Most Brilliant." When I raised my eyes, I saw that all the other girls held a disc, too. Still giggling nervously, they began passing around their awards. Through relief-filled eyes, I read some of their happiness—each disc was inscribed with a unique message of self-worth which had been designed even before the contest had begun. There had never really been a contest! And that was the whole point.

It must have been some creative teacher's idea: to counteract that destructive third grade project of comparing ourselves to each other, to demonstrate in three dimensions that each person has beauty, gifts, and abilities—that there is beauty deeper than the surface and beauty in our differences, not in the fact that we fit into some uniform standard. I don't pretend that I learned that lesson once for all that day, but it was an ordeal-turned-episode to build on. And today, when I rediscovered a small ceramic disc under some papers at the back of a drawer, I felt my face shine with the happy surprise of finding myself valued. I silently thanked the teacher whose name I have forgotten. And I smiled at the memory of an awkward nine-year-old girl who looked into the mirror that teacher held up for her and saw herself as beautiful.

THE SMALL GIFT

Morris Chalfant • Retold by Marilyn K. McAuley

Rev. Chalfant tells of a couple who were celebrating their golden wedding anniversary. The husband was asked what the secret was to his successful marriage. As the elderly are wont to do, the old gentleman answered with a story.

His wife, Sarah, was the only girl he ever dated. He grew up in an orphanage and worked hard for everything he had. He never had time to date until Sarah swept him off his feet. Before he knew it she had managed to get him to ask her to marry him.

After they had said their vows on their wedding day, Sarah's father took the new groom aside and handed him a small gift. He said, "Within this gift is all you really need to know to have a happy marriage." The nervous young man fumbled with the paper and ribbon until he got the package unwrapped.

Within the box lay a large gold watch. With great care he picked it up. Upon close examination he saw etched across the face of the watch a prudent reminder he would see whenever he checked the time of day—words that, if heeded, held the secret to a successful marriage. They were, "Say something nice to Sarah."

Kind words can be short and easy to speak,
but their echoes are truly endless.
Mother Teresa

the beauty and harm

Those are red-letter days in our lives when we meet *people* who thrill us like a fine poem, people whose handshake is brimful of unspoken sympathy, and whose sweet, rich nature impart to our eager, impatient spirits a wonderful restfulness which, in its essence, is divine.

We wake to see with new

eyes and hear with new ears

ny of God's real world

The solemn nothings that fill our everyday life blossom suddenly into bright possibilities.

In a word, while such

friends are near us we

feel that all is well.

-HELEN KELLER

A Debt Of Thanks

Steve Goodier

When William Stidger taught at Boston University, he once reflected upon the great number of unthanked people in his life. Those who had helped nurture him, inspire him, or cared enough about him to leave a lasting impression.

One was a schoolteacher he'd not heard of in many years. But he remembered that she had gone out of her way to put a love of verse in him, and Will had loved poetry all his life. He wrote a letter of thanks to her.

The reply he received, written in the feeble scrawl of the aged, began, "My dear Willie." He was delighted. Now over fifty, bald, and a professor, he didn't think there was a person left in the world who would call him "Willie." Here is that letter:

My dear Willie,

I cannot tell you how much your note meant to me.

I am in my eighties, living alone in a small room, cooking my own meals, lonely, and, like the last leaf of autumn, lingering behind. You will be interested to know that I taught school for fifty years and yours is the first note of appreciation I ever received. It came on a blue-cold morning and it cheered me as nothing has in many years.

Not prone to cry easily, Will wept over that note. She was one of the great unthanked people from Will's past. You know them. We all do. The teacher who made a difference. That coach we'll never forget. The music instructor or Sunday school worker who helped us believe in ourselves. That scout leader that cared.

We all remember people who shaped our lives in various ways. People whose influence changed us. Will Stidger found a way to show his appreciation—he wrote them letters.

Be devoted to one another in brotherly love.

-Romans 12:10, NAS

REMEMBRANCE

Alice Gray • from More Stories for the Heart

er husband died suddenly in an accident and she
was left to raise her two sons alone. At first she
was surrounded by compassionate and caring friends.
They brought meals, sent cards, made phone calls,
prayed. And then the weeks turned into months, and it
seemed like all the world had forgotten. She longed to
hear her husband's name mentioned in conversation,
she longed to talk about the wide stride of his walk, the
warmth of his easy laugh, and how his hand had felt so
strong in hers. She wanted the neighbors to come and
borrow his tools or have a grown man shoot basketballs
with her sons.

It was early on the morning of the first anniversary
of his death. The dew was still wet on the grass as she
walked across the cemetery lawn. And then she saw it,
laying next to his gravestone. Someone had been there

even before her and left a small bouquet of fresh cut flowers, tied with a ribbon. A gentle caring act that reached out to her lonely heart like a tender hug. With tears streaming down her cheeks, she read the unsigned note. The three words said simply, "I remember, too."

A little word in kindness spoken,
A motion or a tear;
Has often healed the heart that's broken,
And made a friend sincere.

DANIEL CLEMENT COLESWORTHY

PRETTIER THAN FRECKLES?

Author unknown

A grandmother and a little girl whose face was sprinkled with bright red freckles spent the day at the zoo. The children were waiting in line to get their cheeks painted by a local artist who was decorating them with tiger paws.

"You've got so many freckles, there's no place to paint!" a boy in the line cried.

Embarrassed, the little girl dropped her head. Her grandmother knelt down next to her.

"I love your freckles," she said.

"Not me," the girl replied.

"Well, when I was a little girl I always wanted freckles," she said, tracing her finger across the child's cheek. "Freckles are beautiful!"

The girl looked up. "Really?"

"Of course," said the grandmother. "Why, just name me one thing that's prettier than freckles."

The little girl peered into the old woman's smiling face.

"Wrinkles," she answered softly.

Pleasant words are a honeycomb, sweet to the soul and healing to the bone.

PROVERBS 16:24, NIV

THE MOST BEAUTIFUL FLOWER

Cheryl L. Costello-Forshey

he park bench was deserted as I sat down to read

Beneath the long, straggly branches of an old willow tree.

Disillusioned by life with good reason to frown,

For the world was intent on dragging me down.

And if that weren't enough to ruin my day,

A young boy out of breath approached me, all tired from play.

He stood right before me with his head tilted down

And said with great excitement, "Look what I found!"

In his hand was a flower, and what a pitiful sight,

With its petals all worn—not enough rain, or too little light.

Wanting him to take his dead flower and go off to play,

I faked a small smile and then shifted away.

But instead of retreating he sat next to my side

And placed the flower to his nose and

declared with overacted surprise,

"It sure smells pretty and it's beautiful, too.

That's why I picked it; here, it's for you."

The weed before me was dying or dead.

Not vibrant of colors, orange, yellow or red.

But I knew I must take it, or he might never leave.

So I reached for the flower, and replied, "Just what I need."

But instead of him placing the flower in my hand,

He held it midair without reason or plan.

It was then that I noticed for the very first time

That weed-toting boy could not see — he was blind.

I heard my voice quiver, tears shone like the sun

As I thanked him for picking the very best one.

"You're welcome," he smiled, and then ran off to play,

Unaware of the impact he'd had on my day.

I sat there and wondered how he managed to see

A self-pitying woman beneath an old willow tree.

How did he know of my self-indulged plight?

Perhaps from his heart, he'd been blessed with true sight.

Through the eyes of a blind child, at last I could see

The problem was not with the world; the problem was me.

And for all of those times I myself had been blind,

I vowed to see the beauty in life, and

appreciate every second that's mine.

And then I held that wilted flower up to my nose,

And breathed in the fragrance of a beautiful rose,

And smiled as I watched that young boy, another weed in his hand,

About to change the life of an unsuspecting old man.

For love is a flower that grows in any soil, works its sweet miracles undaunted by autumn frost or winter snow, blooming fair and fragrant all the year and *blessing those who give* and those who receive.

-Louisa May Alcott

HOPEFULLY SOON

Rochelle M. Pennington

A young mother who had been diagnosed with a treatable form of cancer returned home from the hospital self-conscious about her physical appearance and loss of hair following radiation. Upon sitting down on a kitchen chair, her son appeared quietly in the doorway studying her curiously. As his mother began a rehearsed speech to help him understand what he was seeing, the boy came forward to snuggle in her lap. Intently, he laid his head to her chest and just held on. As his mother was saying, "And sometime, hopefully soon, I will look the way I used to, and then I'll be better," the boy sat up thoughtfully. With six-year-old frankness he simply responded, "Different hair. Same old heart."

His mother no longer had to wait for "sometime, hopefully soon" to be better. She was.

WHEN YOU THOUGHT I WASN'T LOOKING

Mary Rita Schilke Korzan

When you thought I wasn't looking, I saw you hang my first painting on the refrigerator, and I wanted to paint another one.

When you thought I wasn't looking, I saw you feed a stray cat, and I thought it was good to be kind to animals.

When you thought I wasn't looking, I saw you make my favorite cake just for me, and I knew that little things are special things.

When you thought I wasn't looking, I heard you say a prayer, and I believed there is a God I could always talk to.

When you thought I wasn't looking, I felt you kiss me good night, and I felt loved.

When you thought I wasn't looking, I saw tears

Nothing is so infectious as example

-CHARLES KINGSLEY

come from your eyes, and I learned that sometimes things hurt, but it's all right to cry.

When you thought I wasn't looking, I saw that you cared, and I wanted to be everything that I could be.

When you thought I wasn't looking, I looked…and wanted to say thanks for all the things I saw when you thought I wasn't looking.

ROOTS AND WIND

Charles R. Swindoll

I f your life is windy these days —

winds of change, winds of adversity,

or maybe the constant winds of demands and expectations

that leave you feeling, well…windblown —

take heart.

As my mother used to say,

"The roots grow deep when the winds are strong."

DAISY CAKE

Ellen Javernick • from The Christian Reader

It was the most beautiful cake in the world. I was seven then, but I still remember it well. Mother and I baked it together. I got to break the eggs and measure the sugar. I greased the pans carefully so the cakes wouldn't stick. We stirred the batter hard. We didn't want the cakes to be lumpy. Then Mother put the pans in the oven to bake. I set the timer. Mother went upstairs to fold clothes, while I sat at the kitchen table and made Daddy's birthday card. The cake was for him and it was going to be perfect.

The timer hadn't rung yet, but I couldn't wait any longer. I opened the oven for just one peek. The cakes were beautiful—rounded on the top and golden brown on the edges. Just then I heard Mother coming down the stairs. I felt a bit guilty about peeking so I quickly slammed the oven door. The slam came at just the wrong time. The still soft centers of both layers collapsed. When Mom opened the oven door a few minutes later, our beautiful cakes looked like soup bowls.

I cried uncontrollably. Our wonderful surprise was ruined!

"Well, let's see," said Mother, matter of factly, over my sobs. "What can we do about these funny looking cakes?" She began by making the frosting. "White will look nice," she commented. I watched as she turned out the layers onto the cooling racks. "Look how perfectly they've come out of the pans."

I had to admit that was one good thing, but I pointed out that there was still a giant valley in the center of the cakes.

"You're right," said Mother. "I'll just take out this whole center part." She gave us both a taste and we agreed that it tasted yummy.

"But it still looks awful," I persisted. Mother wasn't discouraged yet.

"You run outside and pick some daisies," she said, "while I put the layers together and spread the frosting."

When I returned with the flowers, the freshly frosted cake really didn't look too bad. "Now," said Mother, taking a jelly jar from the cupboard, "we'll just put the daisies in the hole in the center. There—now what do you think?"

"It's the most beautiful cake in the world," I said.

I've never forgotten my mother's lesson. Life is not always full of perfectly rounded golden brown cakes or of perfect days. But we don't have to live with failures; just face them and change them into successes. It works if you're seven or seventy-seven.

If I were you I would not worry. Just make up your mind to do better when you get another chance, and be content with that.

-BEATRICE HARRADEN

A glad giver takes but little
heed of the things that he gives, but all
his desire and

intent is to please

and solace him to whom he gives it. And
if the receiver takes the gift highly and
thankfully, then the courteous giver sets
at nought all his cost and travail, for joy
and delight, that he has pleased and
solaced him that he loves.

-Lady Julian of Norwich

HEIRLOOM

Ann Weems; Retold by Alice Gray • from More Stories for the Heart

had belonged to Great-grandmother and he knew he must be very careful. The vase was one of mother's dearest treasures. She had told him so.

The vase, placed high on the mantle, was out of the reach of little hands, but somehow he managed. He just wanted to see if the tiny little rosebud border went all around the back. He didn't realize that a boy's five-year-old hands are sometimes clumsy and not meant to hold delicate porcelain treasures. It shattered when it hit the floor, and he began to cry. That cry soon became a sobbing wail, growing louder and louder. From the kitchen his mother heard her son crying and she came running. Her footsteps hurried down the hall and came around the corner. She stopped then, looked at him, and saw what he had done.

Between his sobs, he could hardly speak the words, "I broke…the vase."

And then his mother gave him a gift.

With a look of relief, his mother said "Oh, thank heavens, I thought you were hurt!" And then she held him tenderly until his sobbing stopped.

She made it very clear—he was the treasure. Though now a grown man, it is a gift he still carries in his heart.

Riches without charity are nothing worth.
They are a blessing only to him who make
them a blessing to others.
-HENRY FIELDING

Every Minute

Cecil G. Osborne • from God's Little Instruction Book for Dads

erhaps once in a hundred years a person

may be ruined

by excessive praise,

But surely once every minute

someone dies inside for lack of it.

Your words came just when needed.

Like a breeze, blowing and bringing from the

wide salt sea some cooling spray, to a meadow

scorched with heat…and brought new life

and strength to blade and bloom. So

words of thine came over miles to me.

Fresh from the mighty sea, a true

friend's heart, and brought me

hope, and strength, and swept

away the dusty webs that human

spiders spun across my path. So

few there are who reach like thee, and

give the clasp when most its need is felt.

Friend…accept my full heart's thanks.

-ELLA WHEELER WILCOX

NIGHTTIME TREASURES

from God's Little Devotional Book

wo brothers farmed together. They lived in separate houses on the family farm, but met each day in the fields to work together. One brother married and had a large family. The other lived alone. Still, they divided the harvest from the fields equally.

One night the single brother thought, *My brother is struggling to support a large family, but I get half of the harvest.* With love in his heart, he gathered a box of things he had purchased from his earnings—items he knew would help his brother's family. He planned to slip over to his brother's shed, unload the basket there, and never say a word about it.

The same night, the married brother thought, *My brother is alone. He doesn't know the joys of a family.*

Out of love, he decided to take over a basket with

a quilt and homemade bread and preserves to "warm" his brother's house. He planned to leave the items on his porch and never say a word.

As the brothers stealthily made their way to each other's home, they bumped into one another. They were forced to admit to what they were doing, and there in the darkness they cried and embraced, each man realizing that his greatest wealth was a brother who respected and loved him.

You will find, as you look back upon your life, that the moments when you have really lived are the moments you have done things in the spirit of love.

-Henry Drummond

ACKNOWLEDGMENTS

A diligent search has been made to trace original ownership, and when necessary, permission to reprint has been obtained. If I have overlooked giving proper credit to anyone, please accept my apologies. Should any attribution be found to be incorrect, the publisher welcomes written documentation supporting correction for subsequent printings. For material not in the public domain, grateful acknowledgment is given to the publishers and individuals who have granted permission for use of their material.

Acknowledgments are listed by story title in the order they appear in the book. For permission to reprint any of the stories please request permission from the original source listed below.

"Beauty Contest" by Allison Harms, freelance writer, Lake Oswego, OR. © 1997. Used by permission of the author.

"The Small Gift" by Morris Chalfant. Used by permission of the author.

"A Debt of Thanks" by Steve Goodier, author of a

free internet newsletter, Your Life Support System at www.lifesupportsystem.com. © 1999. Used by permission of the author.

"Remembrance" by Alice Gray taken from *More Stories From the Heart*, Multnomah Publishers, Inc. © 1997. Used by permission of the author.

"The Most Beautiful Flower" by Cheryl L. Costello-Forshey. © 1998. Cheryl's poetry can be found in several of the Chicken Soup for the Soul books, *A 4th Course, A 5th Portion, Teenage Soul II, College Soul,* and *Teenage Soul III,* as well as the books, *Stories for a Teen's Heart* and *Stories for a Faithful Heart.* Cheryl's e-mail address is costello-forshey@1st.net . Used by permission of the author.

"Hopefully Soon" by Rochelle M. Pennington, newspaper columnist and contributing author to *Stories for the Heart, Chicken Soup for the Soul,* and *Life's Little Instruction Book.* You may contact her at N1911 Double D Rd., Campbellsport, WI 53010, (902) 533-5880. Used by permission of the author.

"When You Thought I Wasn't Looking" by Mary

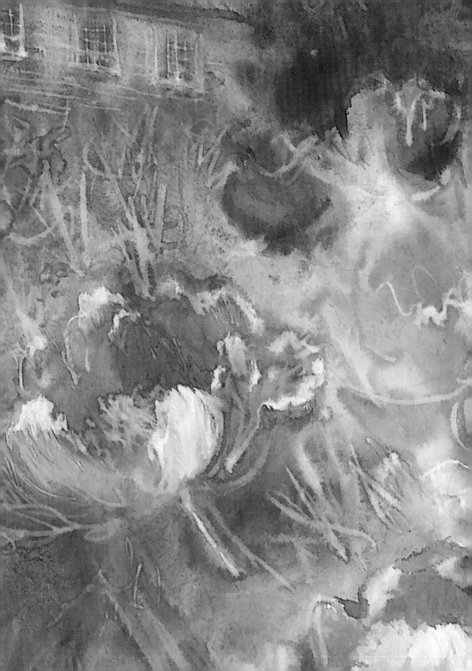